TAMPA BAY BUCCANEERS · SUPER BOWL CHAMPIONS

XXXVII, JANUARY 26, 2003

48-21 VERSUS OAKLAND RAIDERS

SUPER BOWL CHAMPIONS

TAMPA BAY BUCCANEERS

AARON FRISCH

CREATIVE EDUCATION

COVER: LINEBACKER DERRICK BROOKS

PAGE 2: WIDE RECEIVER IKE HILLIARD RUNNING AFTER A CATCH

RIGHT: RUNNING BACK WARRICK DUNN CARRYING THE BALL

Published by Creative Education
P.O. Box 227, Mankato, Minnesota 56002
Creative Education is an imprint of The Creative Company
www.thecreativecompany.us

Book and cover design by Blue Design (www.bluedes.com)
Art direction by Rita Marshall
Printed by Corporate Graphics in the United States of America

Photographs by Alamy (Andre Jenny), Dreamstime (Rosco),
Getty Images (Al Bello, Jonathan Ferrey, Wesley Hitt, Andy
Lyons/Allsport, Al Messerschmidt, Al Messerschmidt/NFL,
Ronald C. Modra/Sports Imagery, Michael Montes/NFL,
Peter Muhly/AFP, Lynn Pelham//Time & Life Pictures, Joe
Robbins)

Library of Congress Cataloging-in-Publication Data

Frisch, Aaron.
Tampa Bay Buccaneers / by Aaron Frisch.
p. cm. — (Super Bowl champions)
Includes index.
Summary: An elementary look at the Tampa Bay Buccaneers
professional football team, including its formation in 1976,
most memorable players, Super Bowl championship, and
stars of today.
ISBN 978-1-60818-029-5
1. Tampa Bay Buccaneers (Football team)—Juvenile
literature. I. Title. II. Series.

GV936.T35F75 2011
796.332'640975965—dc22   2010001026

CPSIA: 040110 PO1141

First Edition
9 8 7 6 5 4 3 2 1

CONTENTS

Tampa Bay is a large harbor on the coast of Florida. A city called Tampa is next to the harbor. Tampa has a stadium called Raymond James Stadium that is the home of a football team called the Buccaneers.

... GAMES AT RAYMOND JAMES STADIUM ARE USUALLY WARM ...

BUCCANEERS FACTS

First season:
1976

Conference/division:
National Football Conference, South Division

Super Bowl championship:
XXXVII, January 26, 2003
48-21 versus Oakland Raiders

Training camp location:
Tampa, Florida

NFL Web site for kids:
http://nflrush.com

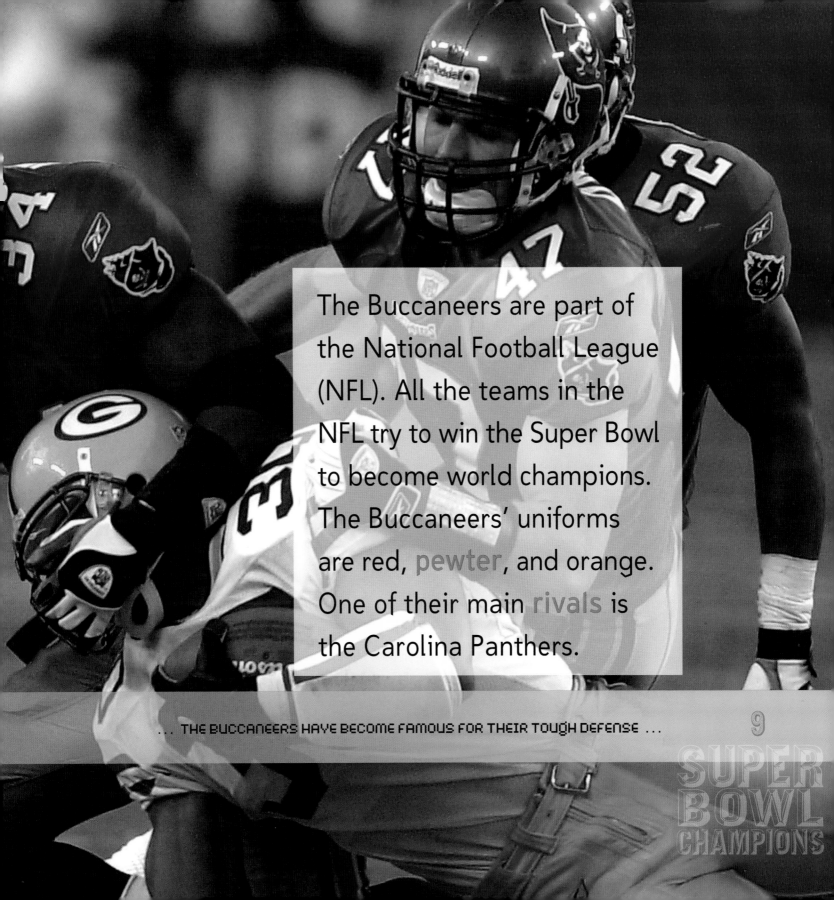

The Buccaneers are part of the National Football League (NFL). All the teams in the NFL try to win the Super Bowl to become world champions. The Buccaneers' uniforms are red, pewter, and orange. One of their main rivals is the Carolina Panthers.

SUPER BOWL CHAMPIONS

The Buccaneers played their first season in 1976. They were so bad that they lost their first 26 games in a row! But players like strong defensive end Lee Roy Selmon helped the Buccaneers get better.

... RUNNING BACK RICKY BELL (LEFT) AND LEE ROY SELMON (RIGHT) ...

SUPER
BOWL
CHAMPIONS

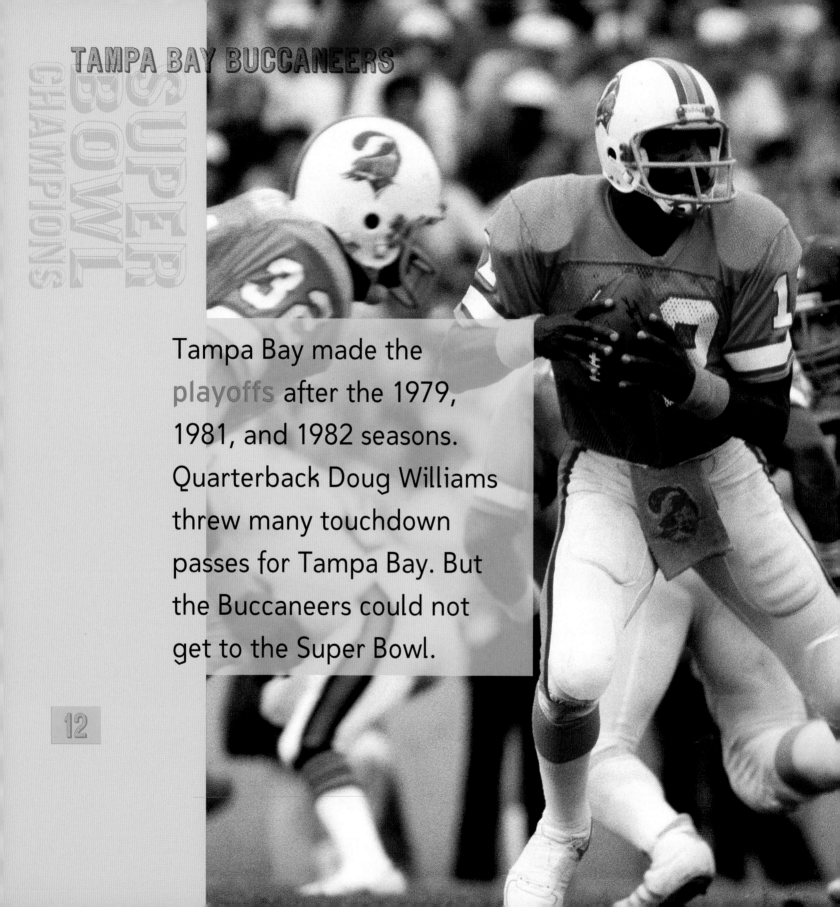

Tampa Bay made the playoffs after the 1979, 1981, and 1982 seasons. Quarterback Doug Williams threw many touchdown passes for Tampa Bay. But the Buccaneers could not get to the Super Bowl.

12

SUPER BOWL CHAMPIONS

The Buccaneers had the best defense in the NFL in the 1990s. Fans cheered for new stars like fast linebacker Derrick Brooks. The Buccaneers got to the playoffs four more times but lost every year.

SUPER BOWL CHAMPIONS

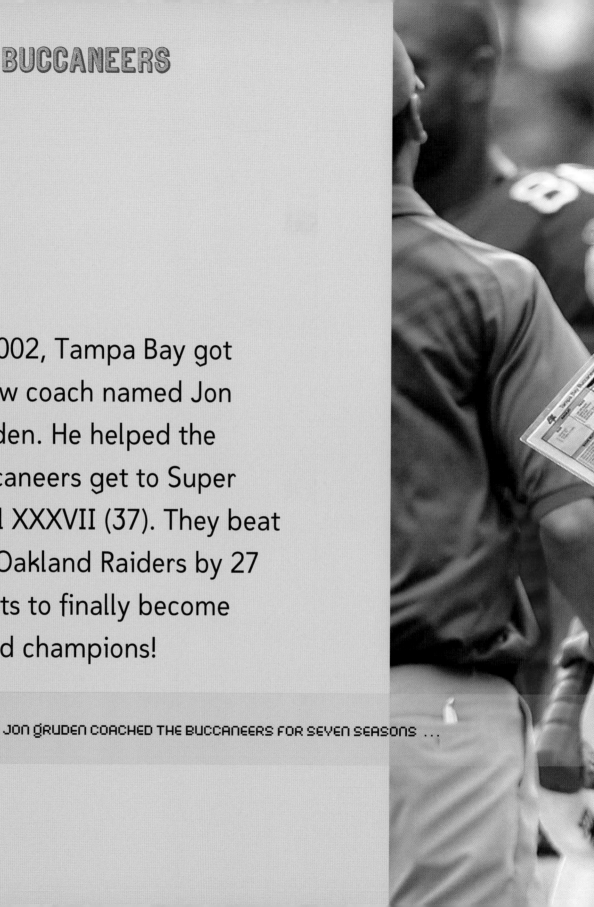

In 2002, Tampa Bay got a new coach named Jon Gruden. He helped the Buccaneers get to Super Bowl XXXVII (37). They beat the Oakland Raiders by 27 points to finally become world champions!

... JON GRUDEN COACHED THE BUCCANEERS FOR SEVEN SEASONS ...

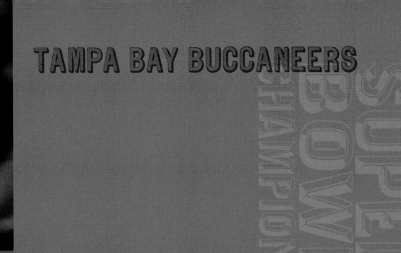

SUPER BOWL CHAMPIONS

The Buccaneers have had many stars. James Wilder was a tough running back who rushed for 13 touchdowns in 1984. Safety John Lynch played for Tampa Bay for 11 years. He was famous for his hard hits.

WHY ARE THEY CALLED THE BUCCANEERS?

Hundreds of years ago, pirates sailed on the ocean by Tampa Bay. Pirates are tough sailors who try to steal treasure. Buccaneers is another name for pirates.

Say It Like This

Alstott:

AHL-staht

ike Alstott and Warrick Dunn were Buccaneers stars, too. They were running backs in the 1990s. Alstott was big and powerful. Dunn was small and quick. Fans called them "Thunder and Lightning."

... MIKE ALSTOTT SCORED 71 TOUCHDOWNS PLAYING FOR TAMPA BAY ...

19

Say It Like This

Ruud:
ROOD

The Buccaneers added linebacker Barrett Ruud in 2005. He led Tampa Bay's defense with 107 tackles in 2009. Tampa Bay fans hoped that he would help lead the Buccaneers to their second Super Bowl championship!

... BARRETT RUUD WAS A LEADER ON THE BUCCANEERS DEFENSE ...

SUPER BOWL CHAMPIONS

GLOSSARY

harbor — a place along an ocean or big lake where ships can stop and stay

pewter — a color that is shiny gray

playoffs — games that the best teams play after a season to see who the champion will be

rivals — teams that play extra hard against each other

stadium — a large building that has a sports field and many seats for fans

23

INDEX